Author's

This book features 100 influential and inspiring quotes by Marcus Aurelius. Undoubtedly, this collection will give you a huge boost of inspiration.

1

"The best answer to anger is silence."

2

"The more we value things outside our control, the less control we have."

3

"It is not events that disturb people, it is their judgements concerning them."

4

"To live a good life: We have the potential for it. If we can learn to be indifferent to what makes no difference."

5

"To love only what happens, what was destined. No greater harmony."

6

"The soul becomes dyed with the color of its thoughts."

7

"Receive without conceit, release without struggle."

8

"Life is short. That's all there is to say. Get what you can from the present – thoughtfully, justly."

9

"Be content to seem what you really are."

10

"How soon will time cover all things, and how many it has covered already."

11

"Each of us needs what nature gives us, when nature gives it."

12

"Remember: Matter. How tiny your share of it. Time. How brief and fleeting your allotment of it. Fate. How small a role you play in it."

13

"Nothing natural is evil."

14

"When someone is properly grounded in life, they shouldn't have to look outside themselves for approval."

15

"He who follows reason in all things is both tranquil and active at the same time, and also cheerful and collected.."

16

"A rock is thrown in the air. It loses nothing by coming down, gained nothing by going up."

17

"If someone responds to insult like a rock, what has the abuser gained with his invective?"

18

"Stick to what's in front of you –
idea, action, utterance."

19

"Be tolerant with others and strict with yourself."

20

"The first step: Don't be anxious. Nature controls it all."

21

"The second step: Concentrate on what you have to do. Fix your eyes on it. Remind yourself that your task is to be a good human being; remind yourself what nature demands of people. Then do it, without hesitation, and speak the truth as you see it. But with kindness. With humility. Without hypocrisy."

22

"Don't be overheard complaining... Not even to yourself."

23

"Do not be perturbed, for all things are according to the nature of the universal; and in a little time you will be nobody and nowhere."

24

"True good fortune is what you make for yourself. Good fortune: good character, good intentions, good actions."

25

"Let not your mind run on what you lack as much as on what you have already."

26

"Objective judgement, now, at this very moment. Unselfish action, now, at this very moment. Willing acceptance, now, at this very moment – of all external events. That's all you need."

27

"How ridiculous and how strange to be surprised at anything which happens in life."

28

"You're subject to sorrow, fear, jealousy, anger and inconsistency. That's the real reason you should admit that you are not wise.

29

"Almost nothing material is needed for a happy life, for he who has understood existence"

30

"For God's sake, stop honouring externals, quit turning yourself into the tool of mere matter, or of people who can supply you or deny you those material things."

31

"As the same fire assumes different shapes when it consumes objects differing in shape, so does the one self take the shape of every creature in whom he is present."

32

"A man when he has done a good act, does not call out for others to come and see, but he goes on to another act, as a vine goes on to produce again the grapes in season."

33

"Receive without pride, let go without attachment."

34

"When you have assumed these names – good, modest, truthful, rational, a man of equanimity, and magnanimous – take care that you do not change these names; and if you should lose them, quickly return to them."

35

"I have often wondered how it is
that every man loves himself
more than all the rest of men,
but yet sets less value on his
own opinions of himself than on
the opinions of others."

36

"Be content with what you are, and wish not change; nor dread your last day, nor long for it."

37

"Receive wealth or prosperity without arrogance; and be ready to let it go."

38

"In a word, if there is a god, all is well; and if chance rules, do not also be governed by it."

39

"So I look for the best and am prepared for the opposite."

40

"Treat whatever happens as wholly natural; not novel or hard to deal with; but familiar and easily handled."

41

"You have power over your mind – not outside events. Realize this, and you will find strength."

42

"Very little is needed to make a happy life; it is all within yourself, in your way of thinking."

43

"Today I escaped anxiety. Or no, I discarded it, because it was within me, in my own perceptions – not outside."

44

"If it's not right, don't do it. If it's not true, don't say it."

45

"The best revenge is not to be like your enemy."

46

"Accept the things to which fate binds you, and love the people with whom fate brings you together, but do so with all your heart."

47

"Confine yourself to the present."

48

"Straight, not straightened."

49

"When you arise in the morning, think of what a precious privilege it is to be alive – to breathe, to think, to enjoy, to love."

50

"Whatever happens to you has been waiting to happen since the beginning of time."

51

"That which is not good for the bee-hive cannot be good for the bees."

52

"To live happily is an inward power of the soul."

53

"You can commit injustice by doing nothing."

54

"Waste no more time arguing about what a good man should be. Be one."

55

"Do every act of your life as if it were your last."

56

"It is not death that a man should fear, but he should fear never beginning to live.

57

"Keep at it... As a blazing fire takes whatever you throw on it, and makes it light and flame."

58

"Dwell on the beauty of life.
Watch the stars, and see
yourself running with them."

"Look well into thyself; there is a source of strength which will always spring up if thou wilt always look."

60

"When jarred, unavoidably, by circumstance, revert at once to yourself and don't lose the rhythm more than you can help. You'll have a better grasp of harmony if you keep going back to it."

61

"If you are distressed by anything external, the pain is not due to the thing itself, but to your estimate of it; and this you have the power to revoke at any moment."

62

"Take the shortest route, the one that nature planned – to speak and act in the healthiest way. Do that, and be free of pain and stress, free of all calculation and pretention."

63

"It's time you realized that you have something in you more powerful and miraculous than the things that affect you and make you dance like a puppet."

64

"The first rule is to keep an untroubled spirit. The second is to look things in the face and know them for what they are."

65

"Keep reminding yourself of the way things are connected, of their relatedness. All things are implicated in one another and in sympathy with each other. This event is the consequence of some other one. Things push and pull on each other, and breathe together, and are one."

66

"As if you had died and your life had extended only to this present moment, use the surplus that is left to you to live from this time onward according to nature."

67

"There were two vices much blacker and more serious than the rest: lack of persistence and lack of self-control... persist and resist."

68

"The universal order and the personal order are nothing but different expressions and manifestations of a common underlying principle."

69

"Look within. Within is the foundation of good, and it will ever bubble up, if you will ever dig."

70

"The only wealth which you will keep forever is the wealth you have given away."

71

"Nothing has such power to broaden the mind as the ability to investigate systematically and truly all that comes under thy observation in life."

72

"Forward, as occasion offers. Never look round to see whether any shall note it... Be satisfied with success in even the smallest matter, and think that even such a result is no trifle."

73

"Because a thing seems difficult for you, do not think it impossible for anyone to accomplish."

74

"People with a strong physical constitution can tolerate extremes of hot and cold; people of strong mental health can handle anger, grief, joy and the other emotions."

75

"If you didn't learn these things in order to demonstrate them in practice, what did you learn them for?"

76

"How long will you wait before
you demand the best of yourself,
and trust reason to determine
what is best?"

77

"'I will throw you into prison.'
Correction – it is my body you
will throw there."

78

"When faced with anything painful or pleasurable, anything bringing glory or disrepute, realize that the crisis is now, that the Olympics have started, and waiting is no longer an option; that the chance for progress, to keep or lose, turns on the events of a single day."

79

"In the morning, when you rise unwillingly, let this thought be present: I am rising to the work of a human being."

80

"No man can escape his destiny,
the next inquiry being how he
may best live the time that he
has to live."

81

"Have I been made for this, to lie under the blankets and keep myself warm?"

82

"Do you have reason? I have.
Why then do you not use it?"

83

"'But I get to wear a crown of gold.' If you have your heart set on wearing crowns, why not make one out of roses – you will look even more elegant in that."

84

"Who exactly are these people that you want to be admired by? Aren't they the same people you are in the habit of calling crazy? And is this your life ambition, then – to win the approval of lunatics?"

85

"Consider what men are when they are eating, sleeping, coupling, evacuating, and so forth. Then what kind of men they are when they are imperious and arrogant, or angry and scolding from their elevated place."

86

"Conceal a flaw, and the world
will imagine the worst."

87

"If you learn that someone is speaking ill of you, don't try to defend yourself against the rumours; respond instead with, 'Yes, and he doesn't know the half of it, because he could have said more'."

88

"He who has a vehement desire for posthumous fame does not consider that every one of those who remember him will himself also die very soon."

89

"Let us overlook many things in those who are like antagonists in the gymnasium. For it is in our power, as I said, to get out of the way and to have no suspicion or hatred."

90

"Begin – to begin is half the work, let half still remain; again begin this, and thou wilt have finished."

"It is just charming how people boast about qualities beyond their control. For instance, 'I am better than you because I have many estates, while you are practically starving'; or, 'I'm a consul,' 'I'm a governor,' or 'I have fine curly hair.'"

"How strangely men act. They will not praise those who are living at the same time and living with themselves; but to be themselves praised by posterity, by those whom they have never seen or ever will see, this they set much value on."

93

""A cucumber is bitter." Throw it away. "There are briars in the road." Turn aside from them. This is enough. Do not add, "And why were such things made in the world?""

"Always observe how ephemeral and worthless human things are, and what was yesterday a speck of semen tomorrow will be a mummy or ashes."

95

"Under no circumstances ever say 'I have lost something,' only 'I returned it."

"To do harm is to do yourself harm. To do an injustice is to do yourself an injustice."

97

"Tomorrow is nothing, today is too late; the good lived yesterday."

98

"Misfortune nobly born is good fortune."

99

"If something does not make a person worse in himself, neither does it make his life worse, nor does it harm him without or within."

100

"The present is the only thing of which a man can be deprived, if it is true that this is the only thing which he has, and that a man cannot lose something he does not already possess."

Made in United States
Troutdale, OR
04/24/2024

19403844R10056